John 3:16

"For God so loved the world that He gave his one and only Son, that whoever believes in Him shall not perish but have eternal life."

Copyright © 2020 by Ca'Shanna Williams.
All rights reserved.
No part of this book, including interior design,
cover design, and/or icons, may be reproduced
or transmitted in any form, by any means
(electronic, photocopying, recording, or otherwise)
without prior written permission from the publisher.

*I would like to dedicate this book to my family
that has always supported and encouraged me to keep doing
what pleases God.*

"Uh!Uh...Mom!" yelled Carmen.
"We have never done this before!"

"What do you mean?" said Momma.

"Inviting others to...
Sofa Time," whispered Carmen.

"First time for everything!" chuckled Momma.

Boys and Girls,

Daddy Williams and I would like to tell you something and we hope that you would never forget it.

You are Awesome and have the power of

AWESOMENESS

Awe-Some-ness... Awesomeness!

"You mean I, or we have power like a superhero or something?" asked Trey.

"**Snap out of it Trey,**" yelled Carmen.

"Yes, if you want to put it that way, son!" said Daddy Williams.

Awesomeness means extremely good or great, explained Momma.
We've all been given the power of **Awesomeness.**

Boys and girls, we want to teach you about your

Awesomeness.

AWESOMENESS

You were created in the image of God
Genesis 1:26-27

God our Father in heaven is *amazing* and He created us like unto Himself.

AWESOMENESS

You are fearfully and wonderfully made

Psalm 139: 14

God made you just the way He wanted you to be.
God did not make a mistake when He created you.
He did not want you to be someone else.

Do not think of yourself less than what you were created to be. Be thankful for the life and body He has given you, expressed Momma.

AWESOMENESS

You are loved by God. We love because He first loved us.
1 John 4:19

There is no love greater than God's love, said Daddy Williams.

"Wait just one minute," said Carmen.
"Don't you and Momma love us more?"

"Carmen, we love you **so much**,
but God loves you most...

always remember that," said Daddy Williams.

AWESOMENESS

You can do all things through Christ our Lord and Savior, who gives us strength.

Philippians 4:13

There is nothing that you can't do if you put your mind to it. Work hard and always believe in yourself, said Momma.

AWESOMENESS

You are more than conquerors.
Romans 8:37

To be a conqueror, you must know that you are winners overall.

It's like
BEING A SUPERHERO DEFEATING THE BAD GUYS.

So when trouble comes your way,
you must believe that,
through our Lord and Savior Jesus Christ,

we will not be defeated...
we are winners, stated Daddy Williams.

Well, Boys and Girls,

Now you know the power of your

Awesomeness.

Go Be Awesome Now!!
We have to go. Thanks for joining us for
Sofa Time.

Goodbye Everyone!

Oh No!
Where did Trey go?

Here I am

Hello, my name is
Captain Awesomeness!

www.ingramcontent.com/pod-product-compliance
Lightning Source LLC
LaVergne TN
LVHW072102070426
835508LV00002B/239